VIA FOLIOS 94

Eye to Eye

Poems by Maria Terrone

Eye to Eye

Poems by Maria Terrone

BORDIGHERA PRESS

Library of Congress Control Number: 2014933968.

Cover Art: "Memory Box" containing an eye miniature, circa 1830. Collection of Dr. and Mrs. David A. Skier; photograph by Sean Pathasema.

Author Photo: William Terrone

© 2014 by Maria Terrone

All rights reserved. Parts of this book may be reprinted only by written permission from the author, and may not be reproduced for publication in book, magazine, or electronic media of any kind, except for purposes of literary reviews by critics.

Printed in the United States.

Published by
BORDIGHERA PRESS
John D. Calandra Italian American Institute
25 West 43rd Street, 17th Floor
New York, NY 10036

VIA FOLIOS 94
ISBN 978-1-59954-070-2

ACKNOWLEDGEMENTS

I thank the editors of the following publications where these poems were first published, some under other titles and with different wording.

Atlanta Review, "Trees in Flame," "A Facebook Page in Iran"
Big City Lit, "Hawthorne Court," "Giraffes, Once Dismissed as Mute"
Blueline, "Cardinal"
Briar Cliff Review, "Off-Season"
The Common, "Ferdinandea," "Models & Marie Antoinette: Two Escapes." The Common Dispatches: "Saturday Afternoon on a New York Railroad Platform"
Comstock Review, "The Tunic"
Crab Orchard Review, "A Bronx Story"
The Evansville Review, "Myopia," "Writing the Body"
Ginosko, "Tableau"
Gravida, "The True Intention of Snow"
Green Mountains Review, "Cyborg Anthropologist"
Hawai'i Pacific Review, "Spaccanapoli"
Heliotrope, "Across the Gulf"
The Hudson Review, "BlackBerry Buzzing," "Knives"
Italian Americana, "Similes in Late August, 2011"
The Ledge, "Deep Inside Our Camera, We're Still Whispering," "Flight"
Newtown Literary, "E.R.," "The Manicurists"
Notre Dame Review, "Eye to Eye," "Travels Inside a Cloister Off Ninth Avenue," "Two Doors"
Paterson Literary Review, "Anew"
Pirene's Fountain, "Vase of Tears," "Words to Unpin Yourself From the Wall," "To Suspend Your Life for Another," "Introducing the Forest to Vivaldi"
Ploughshares, "A Hologram State of Mind"
Poemeleon, "Missing the Names"
Poet Lore, "The Day After," "The Diarist"
Poetry International, ""From Where I Sit," "When the Butcher's Son Passed Me"
Quiddity, "In Hiding"
The Same, "Distance Learning," "Reunion," "On New Year's Eve"
Santa Clara Review, "The Gargoyles Rebel"
SRPR (Spoon River Poetry Review), "Happiness Viewed Through Wings and a White Mask"
2 Bridges Review, "Erased from the Permanent Record" (forthcoming 2014), "The Bath," "Envying the Birds"
VIA (Voices in Italian Americana), "To Begin Again," "Becoming Silver"
Willow Review, "Now a Chill Replaces the Light"

Women's Review of Books, forthcoming, "Radiation Room," "Frigid the Room of Blue Light"

ANTHOLOGIES
Eating Her Wedding Dress: A Collection of Clothing Poems, Ragged Sky Press, "Unmentionable"

Embroidered Stories: Interpreting Women's Domestic Needlework for the Italian Diaspora, University Press of Mississippi (forthcoming 2014), "The Tatted Handkerchief," "Lace"

Sweet Lemons II, International Writings with a Sicilian Accent, "Above the Forests of Second Avenue," "Shorn"

First Water: Best of Pirene's Fountain, "Introducing the Forest to Vivaldi," "Words to Unpin Yourself From the Wall"

"To Suspend Your Life for Another" and "Words to Unpin Yourself From the Wall" were nominated for a Pushcart Prize by *Pirene's Fountain*. "The Manicurists" was nominated by *Newtown Literary*.

I am very grateful to Bordighera Press and Anthony Tamburri, press co-founder and Dean of the John D. Calandra Italian American Institute, for making the publication of this book possible. I also thank Bibi Wein for her keen insight and editorial skill in the preparation of this manuscript, Marie DiRocco for generously giving her valuable feedback as a "first reader," and Joanna Vasquez for her friendship and loyal support from the earliest years of my writing. My appreciation also goes to David and Nan Skier for their graciousness and for enthusiastically providing the *Eye to Eye* cover art.

For Bill
and my late grandmother, Nunzia Felice Marvagna,
and the grandparents never known to me: Domenico Marvagna,
Salvatore Rotondi, and Assunta Marciano Rotondi

Contents

ONE: *Visitations*

Spaccanapoli	19
From Where I Sit	21
Deep Inside Our Camera, We're Still Whispering	22
Tango Room	23
Distance Learning	24
Vase of Tears	25
Eye to Eye	26
Unmentionable	28
Swans' Wake	29
Cave of Forgotten Dreams	30
Cardinal	32
Erased From the Permanent Record	33
Reunion	34
The Lure	35
A Bronx Story	36
Anew	37
The Beach	38
The Visit	39
To Begin Again	40
Off-Season	41
Hawthorne Court	42
Ferdinandea	43
Above the Forests of Second Avenue	45

TWO: *The Body's Way*

Myopia	49
Writing the Body	50
Shorn	52
When the Butcher's Son Passed Me	53
The Day After	54
Radiation Room	55
Words to Unpin Yourself From the Wall	56
BlackBerry Buzzing	57
In Hiding	58

The Bath	59
Country of No Gridlock	60
The Tunic	61
Horsehair	62
To Suspend Your Life for Another	65
Trees in Flame	66
E.R.	67
Envying the Birds	70

THREE: *In Disguise*

Garden of Vogue	73
All But the Serpent	74
42nd Street	75
Becoming Silver	77
The True Intention of Snow	78
Happiness Viewed Through Wings and a White Mask	79
The Diarist	80
The Gargoyles Rebel	81
David's Blade	82
Models & Marie Antoinette: Two Escapes	84
Cyborg Anthropologist	86
Saturday Afternoon on a New York Railroad Platform	87
Plum Island	88

FOUR: *Crossing the Gulf*

Flight	93
Knives	94
The Manicurists	95
Tableau	96
Travels Inside a Cloister off Ninth Avenue	97
Missing the Names	98
The Office	99
Across the Gulf	100
Introducing the Forest to Vivaldi	102
Frigid the Room of Blue Light	103
Lace	104
Similes in Late August, 2011	105

Giraffes, Once Dismissed as Mute	106
A Facebook Page in Iran	107
The Tatted Handkerchief	108
Pastorale	110
On New Year's Eve	112
Two Doors	113
A Hologram State of Mind	114
Now a Chill Replaces the Light	115

Eye to Eye

ONE

Visitations

"Once
a single cell
found that it was full of light
and for the first time there was seeing."

—W.S. Merwin, "Sight"

Spaccanapoli*

I'm a stumbling novitiate here
in jutting shadow, glancing at my watch
when a church bell tolls:
it's 1:15, a time of no apparent meaning,
but the bell resounds, insistent as old men roaring

by on vespas like God almighty, click of stiletto sandals
on Magna Graecia stones, Bulgari jewels that spin
prisms down shop-clotted alleys. Boys joust with friends
and soccer balls in passageways; when doors open
on pot-clatter, then shut, their nail-hung red-pepper rosaries

rise up to knock a blessing. *Ciao! Bella!* Over-ripe vowels
thicken the air; I'm lost in black eyes, as if tumbling
through layers of earth and time into a chamber swelled
by a cult's chants, the tinkling percussion of buried
springs. Chink in the wall! I climb the light

on a spider's thread to rejoin the human web:
vendors crowd basilica steps with offerings
of red shoelaces and hand-carved mangers.
From a sidewalk niche, Neptune lifts his trident
over us all: *Alla vostra salute,* the grime-streaked

gated palazzos; bomb-gouged churches
where bare-shouldered teenage girls kneel
in the glow of Caravaggios; the hidden gardens
sheltering galaxies of lemon trees.
Inside a cloister, 15 marble skulls grin

'round the monk's graveyard plot
(the one wreathed with laurel is laughing),
and I think I could live here with a book
and the happy dead, looking up sometimes to watch
this nun with her radiant rag polishing their heads.

*One of the oldest sections of Naples, center of the original Greco-Roman city of Neapolis.
Alla vostra salute: Here's to you

From Where I Sit

It's possible to move an inch to the left
and see what lies beyond
the half-stripped tree
the birds flee from—the flame tip
of another tree,
the sodium lamp that rises
two stories high, flat head
like a snake. Tonight its light
smears our street yellow.

Do you think I'm a coward
as I move a fraction closer
to the window pane, behind the drape,
watching people rush home from work?
They always leave the frame, entering
a realm I can only imagine: swept up
in this sickly light, propelled
along the pavement like brittle leaves
to end in a heap at their own doorsteps.
Does someone stand on the other side,
ready to open wide?

The dark that has seeped through the slats
now binds my legs.
Maybe they will come soon.
While I wait,
it's possible to move an inch to the right
and see what lies beyond.

Deep Inside Our Camera, We're Still Whispering

Orient, Long Island

We find the creaky-gated burial ground
at Hogpond Farm, crouch and peer in sea-stung air
where swallows beat the sky. No need
to tilt our heads up to see them

when their shadows are more real,
dashing over our hands and the burned grass, bending
to the graves. Chips of flint lie
on each headstone like thumbs on death's eye:

two chips on the white stones of the doctor
and his wife, whose name I share;
fourteen chips on the flat blank stones
of their slaves. The birds cry out

in their soft, high pitch like souls released.
Why did I think we were free?
Inside our camera's black-rimmed frame,
our hushed speech replays
and twittering ghosts still whirl across our feet.

Tango Room

In a dim room at the far end of a long hall,
tiny lights flicker above the dancers—

men and women who learned to tango nights,
after work driving trucks and buffing nails.

They surrender to the body's command,
eyes holding eyes captive, dipping

down and back to music that began
with the immigrants of Buenos Aires,

spread to brothels and dance halls,
now stirring the air of this 19th century hotel room—

unaware of the one who steals a glimpse
from the threshold as they stream

across the dark, wavy mirror on the back wall
like phosphorescent flashes across black water.

Distance Learning

A woman I've never seen
drops by in a dream,
pours a cup of coffee,
pulls up a chair and begins to speak.

I smile, nod, *So true*, refill our cups
again and again. Watching her lips move,
her confidence, I make a mental note:
she is saying so much I must remember,

and though I fail my morning test,
I feel, for the life of me,
changed—awakened by the lessons
of this sage visitor, arrived
from an unnamed country.

Vase of Tears

—Some Mayan vases were used to collect tears at funerals.

And then what?

Did they sip from that tiny cup?
And who—only the one who wailed loudest
or the whole village?

Was a holy woman—
surely it was a woman—
named High Priestess of Tears,
did this Dolores stand guard,
lock them nightly inside a gold vault, cursing
whoever might try to steal grief
to deceive the gods and earn unjust favor?

Was the vase planted in sunlight
so tears could bloom into rain?

Did they water the maize
so all could eat a sweeter daily bread?

Eye to Eye

*Toward the end of the 18th century, portraits of
the single eye of a loved one became fashionable.*
   Exhibit Note, Brandywine River Museum

A mob has been assembled—
just one painted eye per jewelry piece,
but brought together in this glass case,
they feel like the small, still centers

of a hundred hurricanes gathering force, glaring
from pins, pendants, lockets, rings, brooches
framed in gold, encrusted in amethysts
and seed pearls, staring me down,

an eye for an eye. All the rage
in the 18th century: to exchange one of yours
for one of your lover's, to hold the private gaze
beyond the fleeting moment,

so that hazel iris and arched brow,
hint of sideburn or curl can lie
against the other's body for all to see:
love in the eye of every beholder,

like the opera-goers who spied
a gift to the widow from a young Prince of Wales
who started it all—his love a secret
no more. The fashion hit the continent. Imagine

a whole family posing, wide-eyed,
the miniaturist floating their orbs in watercolor
on an ivory box, and friends, cousins,
exchanging platonic glances.

And that German duchess who sent
her daughter off to wed in a foreign land
with a bracelet to watch over her
even after she's gone.   Two tears

of real crystal gleam below the blue eye
of a young man lamenting his own death—
a mourning jewel worn by his bereaved.
Through the glass, he returns my gaze.

•

What does the lover see falling
through that window— to safety, or plummeting
head first? What were you looking at
when we met that made me write,
His eyes penetrate like a laser beam?

As I prepare our dinner, scrubbing away
the film and smell of earth from potatoes,
I think of the disentombed—Lazarus emerging
from the cave, arms raised before that first stab
of light and piercing stares.

You know how hard it must have been for him
to live his life again— always those eyes
riveted on him, wondering what he had seen.

Unmentionable

Buried
at the bottom of my lingerie drawer,
an antique, skin-toned wisp of silk
trimmed with lace and snapping shut
in complicated ways.

A frayed label says
Triangle Shirtwaist Company.

I cannot remember when or how
it came to be here.

I cannot see this confection without
seeing smoke, locked doors and fiery dives
through cruel, unmothering space.

Whose hands cut the silk,
sewed stitches so fine?
Did she hang by a thread for days
to die, or survive,
a wild-eyed girl-child?

This garment I'll never wear
sears me, sighing
from its perfumed vault.

Swans' Wake

The swans have left.

Their single-file parade has rounded
    the lake's corner,

out of view. They avoided
    my gaze as if they bore

beauty's burden, the guilt
    of *brute blood*

and *indifferent beak*
    that let Leda fall.

Such throaty talk among themselves,
    receding.

Such white faces the water lilies raise—
    not flowers strewn

in the swans' wake,
    but a thousand yellow eyes, unblinking.

Cave of Forgotten Dreams

—A Homage to Memory and Werner Herzog

Anything could happen in the Annex,
the above-ground bunker across the yard
from the main school, part of the school
but separate, and that day I felt our isolation
profoundly as I watched the violent rain.
I was one in a class of fifty, girls
in maroon plaid jumpers, boys
in ties and navy pants. No one spoke,
we were hypnotized by the white fury
sweeping towards us,
one obliterating wave after another, alone
with our breathing, a giant clock, and the creak
of wooden desks. The room was sealed,
and dark. I am sure of that, and wonder now
why the nun hadn't turned on the light.
I could make out the oil painting on the back wall,
but dimly, briefly, as if the comfort
of Virgin and Child could be mine only
if I viewed them through a match burning down
between small fingers. Whatever the teacher
may have said has dissolved into mist.
Words didn't matter, or the lessons
learned over a life of seven years—only
the silence of fifty children before
that ravaging rain.

•

Deep inside the bone-strewn
Chauvet caves, home of the oldest wall art,
filmmaker Herzog holds a light to leaping stags,
lions, bulls and one fertile woman,
the only human form. He also looks downward
and ponders the mystery
of footprints—a wolf and a youth, preserved
for millennia, side by side.

Cardinal

Red flits
across the road
as if a bright thought
could not be contained
in the mind's Forest Grimm,
could not be ensnared
by its brambles and thickets,
the dry rot of seasons past.
Feathers fan
the air—fire and bellows—
reigniting
the idea of beauty,
its fury restored.

Erased From the Permanent Record

The music skipped when we hit a bump
in the road. I'd been talking but
we both stopped in the stunning silence—
me mid-sentence, she mid-song.
You kept driving, so the wheels (and earth)
must have continued to spin, and I fell back
to the instant at the chemical plant
that meltdown of a summer when light
like no other—sudden, atomic—pierced
the high, grimy windows, struck
the chrome carriage and metal desk where
I sat, typing—a millisecond's blinding.
And deafening, too, as if
a dome had descended over me
quick as a guillotine, snuffing out
the secretaries' chatter, footfall,
even the other factories' drone.
Then clatter and motion resumed
(snap of a hidden switch) as if
what had happened didn't matter,
and so was struck from time's record.

Reunion

So much white: steam from boiling pots, hair,
teeth—no, bridges—that shine like
phosphorescent paint. And here, and there,
around the table, faces too white above bone
china plates. *So good to see you, so good…*
Can that be Aunt Sunny, who loved
her scotch and smoke, and debonair
Uncle Joe, post-heart surgery, who cuts her food
because she can't see? The couple who loved
to party? A metal fragment pierced
his skull years ago on the job, and now stops
his speech. My godmother is still sharp,
but can't walk, and Dad may know, but probably not,
who's who: his one brother left of the five;
a baby niece called Grace, now white-haired too;
and sister Anna, 82, the same kitchen dervish
I recall from childhood visits
who now pauses to say, *Thank God
we're all here and well.*

The Lure

I can't see the water, but it's near
enough to lift each hair
on my skin—as if, half a mile away,
the sea might still touch me, salt spray
like a vaporous message from the souls
it claimed, the wraiths who dance in foam,
are drawn back, dissolve, re-form.
To be near the sea is to be born
again, to crawl out, then walk,
but also to accept the hook—
to die without thrashing, to slip under and drift
for years, green as a leaf the wind
        pulls from the rest, unmissed.

A Bronx Story

Paralyzed under blankets of steel,
I was pinned to a mattress slab, gray miasma
seeping into my noontime dreams—
the-Bronx-is-burning-to-ashes
light. City-bankrupt-shot-to-hell, always-waning
light. My blank, unemployed mind
slowly woke to awareness, its daily de-enlightenment:
Still out of work. Out of work. Still.

While New York imploded, I baked baguettes,
punched down dough until my fists ached,
watched it rise on a radiator that clanged
victory like a Wall Street bell in better times,
dough doubling and tripling like a wise investment.

Refusing to read a newspaper,
I chopped potatoes for vichyssoise;
keeping down opaque shades, I spooned lightest
crème anglaise into the craters of éclairs I'd beaten
into being with a wooden spoon, pretending
to remember Paris.

Anew

My fingers shriveled from their bath
   of bleach, slips and shirts soaking
in a basin, I think of muslin slapped on stone
   then twisted by swollen hands,
socks squeezed through a mangle,
   and last night's dream: in the back
of an old-fashioned laundry—workers ghosted
by steam—a secret staircase leads me
   to the narrow walkway of a bridge
across Manhattan, that shimmering island
   slyly winking promise.

On the island of Murano, we admired
   the spectrum of T-shirts
posed on clotheslines in buoyant
   Venetian light, and I learned that
it's possible for a body to float
   on joy. At our hotel, your handkerchiefs
and my camisoles were transformed,
   dazzling squares left in a basket
at the door; within, embroidered sheets
   white as baptismal linen.
How easy it was to feel washed clean.

The Beach

In a dream the old white tile
that our feet touched had disappeared,
and in its place, a deep hole.

The sea's obsessive swallowing,
undertow a constant ground shift
beneath me.

Sand shovels abandoned, excavation done,
the children lean into the damp and dark.

People can vanish
like overexposed photos in this blinding.

Better to leave by degree—

a woman painted by Vuillard
whose patterned dress merges
with curtains behind her, or that fraction
of a man's face peering
from the shadowed edge.

At night when you're not here,
the fog comes, and the shape shifting:

tiny pearl shells, translucent
as newborn ears, listening,
and the fixed, glazed eyes
of creeping stones.

The Visit

Bog people unearthed by the claws
of peat machines, preserved a thousand years,
skulls still sprouting hair,
faces contorted, tortured and dumped:
mysteries of a Dublin museum.

And then a pounding at 3 a.m.,
WHAT was THAT? Not a dream,
the banging insistent
against our door with no peephole.
"Why won't you let me in?"
Such a plaintive voice belied by more banging,

imagining the man in trouble,
the man drunk and violent, the man
we learned had dragged his crutches
up and down the hotel hall, battering ram
against baseboards—

like a medieval peasant pursued
by a savage clan who limps back and forth,
leaving dusty furrows
outside the gates of Glendalough,
St. Kevin's walled, monastic city,
wanting in.

To Begin Again

Open the new calendar,
a grid of days,
white boxes like regiments all in order
and accounted for
alert before the Sahara of a new year
time's persistent *sirocco*
that sculpts the meticulous, empty landscape.

Open the New Year to 365 town squares
and close your eyes
to picture the daily *passeggiata*,
how surreal it would be to strut across
the cobblestones alone.

•

In separate squares, people begin
to appear, smoking by a fountain,
sipping espresso, glancing at a watch
that frowns back 8:20,
a.m. or p.m., who knows?

One by one they fill the spaces,
friends, colleagues, cousins.
And slouching at the margins mid-year
those strangers, waiting
for you to show.

Off-Season

Rocks etched like elephants' hides
lumber down a jetty where a sign warns

Keep Off. The tide moves closer,
a whitened fist that opens,

then withdraws. Last month I kissed my father
as he lay, eyes shut, in the hospital bed.

I whispered in his ear a last time,
not knowing. Five bearded, barefoot men

in black suits and hats appear,
streaming towards the sea. And from where

did the two girls in long white dresses come?
They dash across the sand, arms extended,

laughing, as if, despite their lightness,
they had to tunnel through air, whose lash

they've never felt. A boy tugs
at a gull-shaped kite that fights the wind.

Hawthorne Court

The day unfurls for the tourists
who come once a year to the garden
enclosed by brick buildings.

Some exclaim at tiger lilies and iris,
others sit on stone benches to face
the improbable sweep of sunlit lawn

through a lens. Fanned open, the day presents
a scene that's nearly pastoral, serene
despite the muffled hum of the city.

Tonight I'll walk alone here.
Two white cats will scurry away
from my footfall, and the moon will follow them

into the ivy, spilling its milk into their fur.
I'll inhale the scent of rosemary
pinched between my fingers, passing through

corridors of gnarled hawthorn trees that lean
towards me like question marks. Dense, too,
the towering maples, impenetrable

as my dreams; and all the mourning
doves, silent now within the larger sheltering
silence, their wings folded.

Ferdinandea

A ghost island that appeared near Sicily in July 1831

When the buried volcano erupted,
sulfuric smoke leapt from the sea,
seeped through locked, felt-lined chests,
blackening the silverware.

It was like rage—flames and letting go,
the sea a bubbling cauldron of dead fish,
a bad taste in the mouth.
An islet rose from the depths—

not glittering Atlantis, but a desolation
swiftly spreading like news of its strange
arrival. Who can know why four nations
would stake claim to a stark mile

of tufa and pumice, what a naval surgeon called
"unhallowed ground"? Even the gulls fled,
screaming, but not the scientists, dreamers,
adventurers, curiosity-seekers,

cartographers who eyed nearby Tunisia,
and writers seeking mythic inspiration—
Jules Verne, Sir Walter Scott,
James Fenimore Cooper, Alexandre Dumas.

Like a wine connoisseur, someone sipped
the water of its two ponds, lived to pronounce

the red one "salty, spicy,"
the yellow one "sulfuric."

By December, the ghost had vanished
to a smudge of shoal with a new British name.
Soldiers and sailors returned home.
Contessas reclaimed their silver spoons.

Above the Forests of Second Avenue

Her right hand flies up, then plunges down,
the embroidery needle between her bony fingers
like a beak that seeks nourishment,
but can't be filled and must rise to try again.

The needle alights on white cotton
as if to sip nectar or peck a seed,
but can't stay for more than a second.
Far across shining seas

of scrubbed linoleum, we sit—nephews,
nieces, cousins—eating the feast she cooked
while we slept. The needle rises
in a blur, veins on the back of her hand

pulsing like a small bird's heart.
We hardly notice when the flowers appear,
stem, leaf, then bud, and how they spread
across the field that ripples on her lap,

down her legs' spindly trellis, over the cracked plain
of a railroad flat five flights above the forests
of Second Avenue, strewn across an ocean,
back to the hills of Lercara Friddi.

Two

The Body's Way

What is this mask of skin we wear,
What is this dress of flesh...?

—Marge Piercy, "My Mother's Body"

Myopia

Not a diminishing—
the body's way of forcing me
to look closer.

If I lie eye to eye
with these blades of grass,
I may see what they hide:

insect, feather, pebble,
maybe the cameo
that came unpinned

as I walked here decades ago:
that once noble face
framed by wild green hair.

Writing the Body

—On two works by Naomi Grossman
Queens College Art Center Exhibition

Sculpture: "Freefall"

Did the dice tumble, too,
        flung across a table,
   when all her luck ran out?

Or was she a high-flyer
       who dared,
risked all, got burned—
   a female Icarus
      who plunged
        head first into air's gyre,
       holding her last
        breath, breathless
    in the company of heartbeat
     and wing,
earth pulling her
   closer, her fall
into freedom
     giving rise
   to a new mythology.

Altered Photo of Nude: "Holding Myself Together"

Message stroked
across a canvas of flesh,

hieroglyphs on the cave wall
called woman.

Holding herself, she hides
her face, holding
her self, we behold enigma,
work in progress,
woman-in-process.

Behold her becoming what?
A warrior adorned?
Painted by whom? The self
she hides?
Or painted by passers-by?

Behold this painted woman
of fruit-stained lips,
kohl-rimmed eyes,
the face she hides radiant
behind an arm. Maybe.

This naked Eve hides
to save face. Maybe.

Her body speaks
in its twisting

away. We cannot
make out the writing.

Is she holding up,
does the center hold?

We cannot read her.
We make her up.

Shorn

I sell my thick black hair for *lire*.
Why? So a woman who always wants more
can be a *bella donna* who struts
down the street, tossing her head
like an American movie star.

But then I remember the sick woman
who wants to hide
the illness that pulls her by the roots,
to cover her skull sprouting spiky tufts
like land cursed for centuries.

When shivers climb my naked neck,
I take comfort thinking that maybe
it's this woman who wears my hair,
who takes shelter inside it the way, as a girl,
I'd lie for hours inside waves of sea grass.

Note: *Italian hair, prized for its thickness and luster, is used for the most expensive wigs.*

When the Butcher's Son Passed Me

on the street, he was cradling a skinned lamb
in his arms,
stripped to the bone, its head askew.
He held the body
as a blood-splattered father
might hold a child he had just lost,
knowing there is nothing to be done,
his apron a map of sorrow.

The Day After

I fold your shirts neatly into a pile
    on what had been your bed.
        Just below each collar, a white tape

with your name in black indelible
    ink. I run my fingers over the soft
        plaid flannel of your name,

white cotton undershirt of your name,
    loose drawstring sweatpants
        of your name, placing all into the black

plastic bag, along with the leather shoes
    and slippers that rarely touched ground—
        all meant for someone with nothing

to his name, who will wear these garments
    you wore just days ago over flesh
        that still sweated, shivered, rose and fell.

Radiation Room

Here I lie, forced to face the heavens—
a Kodachrome distraction
installed years ago, long-haired young women
in meadows and forests
who move through each framed image,
defined grid of a happy life
faded to sinister blue-green.

No arching of neck needed to marvel
at man and God on a chapel dome,
light streaming.

Two technicians lean over,
carefully adjusting me into a place where
millimeters count
(child chasing a ball into the street,
screeching brakes). The machine

descends close, so close,
blinks its one red eye.

Words to Unpin Yourself From the Wall

You want to be somewhere else, out of
the three-hour lecture, the marathon reading,
out of your pinned skin, inside
the wild commotion of small birds hidden
within a massive tree that seems to swell and vibrate.
To be inside one feathered throat pulsing and the vortex
of autumn leaves pulling the last light to itself.

Tell them you must go, then speak no more. Risk all
for the last leaf and the other-wordly calls at liftoff.
Feel the magnetic imperative of that high,
black string drawn across continents. Stay
until you can't see sky or the upturned face
of the stranger who's joined you,
and it's the wind that has the last word,
blowing sharp leaves at your lips—
such rough, red kisses.

BlackBerry Buzzing

I love the feel against my hip or hand
or handbag. Not just in September, but always,
the buzz like a burr against my body,
slightly prickly, insistent as I stand alone
in a field or on a city street surrounded
by others being buzzed too, summoned,
prodded, wondering Who? Who? and then lifting
the slick, compact, inky-black BlackBerry
to my lips and ear, open to the words that come
tapped or spoken, bidden or unbidden,
satellite-bouncing across hills, valleys, rivers,
leaping over oceans, big sky, skyscrapers,
avenues, alleyways, words I take within me,
sweet-familiar or darkly deep, luscious in any season.

In Hiding

For Li-Young Lee

I stand in the rented lake house
in lamplight, book opened
to the first poem,
"In His Own Shadow,"

see a mosquito's shadow
waver on the page,

and from that shadow,
track its breathing,
track it down to a whack—
our blood mingling on the wall.

I learned long ago
I can hide my body
but not my shadow that spilled
under closet doors where I crouched
with held breath in a child's game,
trying to evade the Seeker,

now trying to evade the day when
my body will be a shadow
ghosting a page
held in another's hand.

The Bath

The slippery promise of jasmine soap
in the curve of my palm: I hush the roaring
spigot and ease into water calm
as dreamless sleep,
the dregs of a day banished
from this purchased, perfumed hour.
Tiny bubbles form and fizzle out,
casting a violet sheen like the after-image
of distant stars just visible
through steaming nebula. How strange
it feels to watch my mind, stripped clean,
drift like a hollow barge until a thought

tumbles out like a smudged note
the broom missed: today she returned.
Trailing a black-patched robe,
she screamed *Unclean*
to all who would hear her confession,
warning, rebuke. Pedestrians clutched
at their lapels, noses tucked within to breathe
the scent of their own skin. When the wind tore
at her newspaper wimple,
she screamed again *Unclean*.
The two red circles painted
on her cheeks deepened to stains.

Country of No Gridlock

Duet of birds hidden
beyond the white, fern-imprinted sky.
    I am grasping
even in this vastness.
Even as I try to leave
my mind's clogged byways behind,
    I am grasping.
To learn how to unclench:
this is what I must do.
To be a small green thing,
unfurling.

        •

Trees encircle the inn's patio,
slope down to the road.
Traffic streams past in this country
of no gridlock;
water spills over stones, polishing them
in its imperceptible
grinding down. Green chair
I sit in. Green table where my book lies,
    face up.
Once you and I lay
in a Vermont meadow,
    facing the sky.

The Tunic

> *"They divided my garments among them and for my vesture they cast lots."*

For once, I was the winner. The tunic was a miracle—
      all of a piece and not one stitch visible,
sturdy enough to withstand cold desert nights
      but a caress on my shoulders, lined
with the finest silk. I would like to meet the woman
      (mother? sister?) who loomed and cut and sewed
this cloak, for only one who greatly loved that man
      would take such tender care. I saw at once
the shabbiness of my own coat and tossed
      it to a passing beggar. He kissed my feet and hands

as if I were divine! Such a strange day it was—
      the mob screaming for his blood, then a rumor
that when the sudden darkness came,
      their temple curtain tore. Who knows the truth?
We wrap ourselves in what helps us endure
      the next wretched day or battle
and cry out to the gods for protection. Me?
      I've come to sleep in my prize:
last year in the tavern, a drunken lout's knife
      did not penetrate or leave the slightest mark.

Horsehair

> *"Some doctors started to notice that patients with horsehair sutures had a lower infection rate than silk. It was widely thought that there was some sort of curative quality derived from horses."*
> —CivilWarTalk.com, "Sergeant Major," Maryland

My husband applied it to my breast
post op, as the surgeon instructed.
I didn't ask why, wondering later about
the healing power of the tassels
on a Reiki drum or shaman's wand.

•

National Velvet: Young girls and the horses they love.
What did I know of all that—petting flanks,
still-small fingers stroking the silky mane?

On the Coney Island Steeplechase, I clung
to the painted stallion who trailed a hank of real hair.
Together, we moved forward on the track,
tracing circles, loving the fast ride, not the horse,
aching thighs a foreshadowing.

•

Yankees and Confederates fallen from their steeds
onto the bloody fields: split by bayonets,
riddled with lead. For some, a redemption

to be sewn with horsehair,
white threads rejoining the divided body.

•

We circled the track into the 21ˢᵗ century,
breast riven, emptied, stuffed, sewed shut,
with what kind of thread I don't know.

The horsehair found me:
white fuzz in a glassine envelope
the doctor handed over. Gossamer
when my husband gripped a few threads
with a tweezer and placed them on my wound.

•

Why during that time did I dream of flight?
I imagine Pegasus streaking across the sky, unbridled,
scattering stars like a cloud of dust.

•

Experience of Dr. W.W. Greene, cited by The Boston
Medical and Surgical Journal, 1867:
"*He has applied the horsehair stitches in almost every
locality, both in the skin and in the mucous membrane,
and has never secured such beautiful, delicate
linear scars with any other article.*"

My linear scar runs along a north-south axis,
angled at the top by the surgeon's knot.
Obscured sometimes by lace: the skin's embossing,
delicate pink track on the body's map.

•

*We are North America's foremost purveyor of the fine quality
unbleached white horsehair for bows of the violin family
as well as black mare and stallion horsehair often used
in bass bows.*

I imagine music coursing through my single breast.

To Suspend Your Life for Another

November wind swoops
   black leaves into its arms
and heaves them
   to the thirteenth floor
where they appear outside this glass
   like a flock of birds, wings useless
as brittle paper. My brain registers
   grackles, each one alone,
pummeling the elemental air,
   then sucked back
into a single furious
   whirl. Once my breath stopped
as two birds in flight
   paused here,
one upside down, beak
   linked to beak,
utterly still, an inked
   illustration stamped on my brain
of all that is possible.

Trees in Flame

A burning needle stitches me
        along the incision,

bisects my breast with its quick piercing,
        a fire insistent as the sight

of these trees. Against
        November rain they assert

with fury their will, their right,
        to dazzle

with this improbable light, even as
        time and wind take without asking.

E.R.

The prisoners from Rikers arrive shackled,
seems like five cops to one.

Their caretakers in blue shoot
the breeze with one another
and their charges—sports mostly,
the usual stuff, and read the *Post*,
check smart phones, poke their mouths
with fries from crackling waxed bags.

•

No life-and-death seesaw here—
the heart-attacked and bullet-ridden
have been whisked away. Hours squeeze
themselves out like a saline drip.
New names appear on the board,
except for "male, i.d. unknown,"
registered at midnight.

•

A patient with a bruised brow
dreams aloud in Chinese.

•

The Denzel Washington-lookalike
shakes his shackle, demands
a "nurse administrator."

Distraction arrives:
a round of thin cheese sandwiches
dispensed with foil-sealed cups of o.j.

•

Three voices behind a curtain, a volley
of Spanish and English. The cop-translator emerges,
his arms a map of vein-blue tattoos—
too dense to distinguish a word.

•

Relentless beeps like a mechanical monster's heart.
The orderly says they've invaded
his sleep, monitoring even his dreams.

•

Behind a guarded door, paroxysms
of coughing. A blond woman in face mask
and handcuffs is led away.

•

Doctors rush about, sitting only to study
computer screens. I watch
what I can't read or know
move down and away, unscrolling like life.

•

2 a.m.: my mother, face bruised from her fall,
signs her discharge forms.

•

The night reels.
More patients are wheeled in.
This negative space is more crowded
than eight hours ago, but now only machines speak.

Some enshroud their heads
with rough muslin sheets, motionless and silent
despite what brought them here.

Envying the Birds

Of course, their flight. How long
      since I dreamed I was one of them,
cruising the neighborhood, marveling
      at winged gargoyles
on apartment building tops?

Next time,
      there will be no learning to crawl,
stumble, walk, fall, break, ache,
      there will be no xrays, scans
of my weightless, hollow bones.

      I'll rise early without effort
or the need to feel virtuous.
      There will be no gurgles,
splutters, baby babble, back talk, wisecracks,
      black-tie speeches, or words
that richochet and fall like spent bullets.

Three

In Disguise

*"The murmur rises, the dark is torn to shreds,
and the shadow you cast on the fragile
trellis wrinkles. Too late
if you wish to be yourself!"*

—Eugenio Montale, "Waterfront"

Garden of Vogue

Strands of wet hair etch both cheeks
    like the cracks on an antique doll,
finer wisps cobweb her brow,
    cinch her neck.
Black waves toss wild against the whorl
    of tree trunk she leans on or lies against—

hard to tell if she's vertical or horizontal,
    if the tree rises or has fallen.
Untamed brows say
    dryad, wood nymph, earth-released, say
Come closer.

And there's her pleated Calvin Klein gown
    imprinted with a pattern of skin or blood
seen through a microscope
    and just below the shoulder, that bruise.

All But the Serpent

She lies face up in a secret place—
   untamed garden or tamed jungle,
no matter. She lies
   with a Louis Vuitton bucket-bag,
its repeating monogram
   like visa stamps to Xanadu. Gold
fringe spills from nowhere, striping
   her pale thigh. A white dove, wings blurred,
balances on raised fingers;
   two more nestle nearby
in the high dried grass. Why these birds,
   this hint of headless
raccoon? Why this dress
   of fuzzy green scraps
that could be plucked for a nest?
   Her browless, half-closed eyes
are no window.
   It's her parted lips that see.

42nd Street

This is the Big Top!
Where else can you eat a Big Mac
in a former vaudeville theater
open to the street,
its carved fleur-de-lis facade
flashing neon,
and face the Children of Paradise
on parade?

Just one block back, I saw a man
        pace, mechanical and mute,
holding a tiny hand-lettered sign,
Comedy Club. He wore combat
boots, not oversized clown shoes,
and avoided his competitor who warned,

    The End is Near.

Slipping inside a chain
cosmetics store big as a hangar,
feeling disembodied,
I wander in the land of lipstick lust,
and come upon a man in a white satin
skullcap and frothy tutu
perched on a stool.

A fine line of black tears is precisely
drawn on his opaque chalk-face,
raised in the hope of help's arrival.

I feel my fingers fly up
to my own face,
like a blind woman.

Becoming Silver

Faces forged to a new coin's hard dazzle,
they stand rigid on hidden stilts
above the piazza, unblinking.
Euros heap in buckets at their feet,
but they gaze only at the horizon,
staking mute claim for another kind

of mother lode, calculating the currency
that rules their odd kingdom,
and even when sweat inscribes a cheek,
it's as if they're still sculpting themselves
and their place apart from the blur
of restless tourists, all the skittering children,

the shadows that creep inside the fountain,
staining the teenagers' skin.
The silver people remain unmoved,
Pygmalions who've tried
to make their own flesh stone,
eternal as the carved guardians of tombs.

The True Intention of Snow

Everywhere
snow wraps
thick bandages
around rickety tree limbs
and the twigs
of sleeping forsythia
that may break
from the weight
of its care.

This snowfall
began with a kiss
on eyelashes,
then toppled power lines,
stranded trucks,
and tricked a woman
who slipped
into its embrace—

first soothing her
like a cloth
on a fevered brow,
then holding on
and on, a balm
of long white strips
that wrapped
her body
like a pharaoh.

Happiness Viewed Through Wings and a White Mask

> *"As a new geisha, I was given a name
> that meant 'transparent happiness.'"*
> —From a women's magazine

The spectrum appears
in a dragonfly's wings
so that if you look closely enough
you'll see the world spread before you
from red to violet.
Maybe that world will take flight
with you along for the ride
and brain and blood will understand
the origin of "sheer joy."

As for the geisha,
trained in genteel conversation,
to pour saki and tea,
to entertain through ceremonial dance—
she smiles at clients
with no hint of complication
through a white mask,
then cinches her indigo obi,
her opaque sash of night.

The Diarist

She could write only with a pencil.
In time the words blurred as if
rebelling against her as if
they did not want anyone,
including her, to read her mind.
She kept writing down her life,
snippets squeezed against
margins, hugging the bars
of spiral notebooks.
The words remained cryptic,
steadfast in their refusals.
Every New Year's Eve,
she hid the past year so well,
even she could not find it.

The Gargoyles Rebel

From their lofty cathedral perches,
activists spread the word:
We will no longer be gutter-slaves,
a conduit for medieval ideas!

They agree to end the boredom
of enforced utility, service with a snarl
unnoticed for centuries by the human crawl

below. Through the next rain,
the gargoyles swallow hard
and then seal tight their mouths,
becoming more like us—

pressured to bursting, cracking,
teetering on the edge.

David's Blade

The fake gold razor blade
you wore around your neck
stopped me cold today,
as I sifted through my jewelry clutter.

I still can't bring myself to watch
"Philadelphia," knowing you
were an extra who didn't need direction
to play a dying man.

In the office, when you admired
my thick chain bracelet, I handed it over
for your gold-tone bauble.
The blade was a joke, of course, accessory
to jeans and gym-pumped muscles,
our impromptu "West Side Story" duets,
"We're gonna rumble
tonight!" in the magazine's hall.

I understood everything the weekend
I encountered you at a Bette Davis
feature. Eyes lowered, you mumbled,
not introducing your boyfriend.
He could have been your twin,
but I doubt he could quote
Lord Byron or recite the names
of every pope since 1500. I loved you.

For years after you left New York,
I'd think I saw you, always turning the corner.

Now you've returned in online obits,
glimpses of your life from that ravaged time,
and a dull mix of fingerprints
that clings to our razor blade.

Models & Marie Antoinette: Two Escapes

Even tight, feared spaces can expand, morphing from the past
into the fuzz of nostalgia, which I'll try to avoid here,
e.g. #1, me at 16, looking for the "model studio" listed
in the Manhattan Yellow Pages. Toting a portfolio, I climb
the stairs of a West 40s walkup worn as another century.
"Models?" "No, that's Cheekie, 2 flights up,"
one red talon points to heaven and off I go.
A woman in a sheer negligee greets me, opens the door wider:
I take in a stripped-bare space, commercial buzz, the motion
of flouncing baby dolls, lace bra the black center
of a blinding white circle, and Cheekie, I assume,
behind the tripod. The image flickers across my retina,
then burns in. The hallway presses close, and my skin feels tight,
as if about to chip off in jagged bits like the ancient green paint.
I flew from there—no, plunged—a bird escaping fire.

e.g., #2, someone lit matches after the creaky elevator cable
snapped and plunged its human load
that New Year's Eve in SoHo. I believe
it was Marie Antoinette in drag. I remember her coiffure,
towering ice sculpture frozen to perfection,
and satin billows that regally occupied half the elevator,
brushing against the perturbed ventriloquist who clutched
his dummy tighter. Neither had spoken all night, stopping
conversation instead with their sudden appearance and stares
in the center of happy talkers. Yes, I'm certain it was the Queen
who struck matches from a book hidden in décolletage,
holding up each brief, tiny flame like a torch, guiding us

once we hit bottom—jarred but not hurt—feeling
our way through the pitch of a basement
that could have been a Bastille dungeon, but wasn't.

Cyborg Anthropologist

She might bleed on her readers—
an occupational hazard from riding culture's cutting
edge, for understanding what it means for humans
and objects to interact. I don't.
Understand, that is. Though I do interact
all crazy hours of the day and night, but more
from addiction than fondness for my ipad.
She purveys ideas that Descartes
would have considered:
smart phones thinking and therefore being.
In her *National Geographic* photo,
she looks almost too human, vulnerable,
with that prim peter-pan collar and nursery-school
bangs worn probably with irony, as if to say,
 *I am too young to remember the past
so I wear the look of an ancient time, maybe your time—
when chatting on a turquoise Princess phone
was to be tethered by its cord to a future
you thought you could imagine.
But you were wrong.*

Saturday Afternoon on a New York Railroad Platform

The National Guard is on patrol
in combat boots and GI Joe camouflage,
M16's slung down to their hips,
young as boys on Halloween,
ready for anything, and I want
to hand every one of them a bag of candy.

Teens heading home from the shore
jostle one another, breaking
into impromptu dance; sparkles scatter
across a girl's grass-green miniskirt
like dew. It's Morning in America.
Her friend lifts a Coke
from a canvas tote striped red, white and blue,
and gulps deeply, head wrapped
in a star-spangled do-rag.
Wind swells his Yankees T-shirt
like a schooner's sail,
shakes his gold hoop earring.
A squall is coming on.

I lean over the track, pretending
to be fearless. Two cops glide past:
one, freckled and pink-cheeked,
his black partner middle-aged-weary,
like Huck Finn and Jim heading to
wherever the river takes them.

Plum Island

A government research center in Long Island Sound

Think germ warfare,
pathogens, deformed animals washing ashore
from Hannibal Lecter's favorite hot spot.
Think conspiracy: a former Nazi
paid by the CIA to develop Lyme disease.
Sweep your binoculars across its three miles;
see the low-slung bunkers approachable only
by boat with Homeland Security clearance.
Or spy online for what it's worth. Note
the work of Lab 257, denied, then exposed,
forced to shutter.

The waters of the Sound sparkle
like splintered glass around the island, daring
the curious. How to understand such beauty?
Return in your mind's eye
to the jasmine-perfumed hike you took
to view Plum from Orient Point—a corridor
of fuschia-daubed bushes and waves breaking
over a beach strewn with bone-smooth
driftwood. A "wish you were here" scene

until you near the tip and come upon
a pole-mounted camera eyeing you
from behind a wire cage. Wave,
but Keep Off if you haven't noticed.
Now look down: black cables thick and thin

burrow below ground, then stretch
across the channel. They power the island
and send knowledge back and forth, undulating
unseen like snakes in a lidded basket.

Four

Crossing the Gulf

*I've been watching
an evening star quiver. I've been trying
to identify the word before its utterance.*

—Stephen Dunn
"The Snowmass Cycle"

Flight

I grew up in a desert, where

    parachutists floated

past my window,

    common as tumbleweed.

Sometimes I stood outside

    watching specks of men

become the centers

    of wild orchids opening.

I knotted together stories

    as if they were sheets dropped

from a small, high window.

    I imagined where they were bound

and felt one foot, then the next,

    touch down like drops of rain.

Knives

> *"In most kitchens all over Jerusalem or Tel Aviv, there are Palestinians and Israelis cooking together, shoulder to shoulder, with long knives."*
> —A Chef for Peace, quoted in *The New York Times*

Sulphured air, the fire
beneath convulsing pots,
sudden roar of jets
igniting. Sweat of bodies
whirling in chaotic space,
blunt impact, flying shards.
Orders shouted through tents
of steam.

But the only blood here
is the lamb's as it pools
on a scarred plank.

The knives,
crossed daily against
ancient stone,
keep to themselves.

The Manicurists

Kim, the owner, trills
a greeting through her mask,
points to a table set with a paper placemat,
rose-scented water in a painted porcelain bowl,
gleaming metal implements.

All speak the same tongue
and each twitter flutters up
to the fluorescent lights
as swallows flock to a barn's eaves.

I splay my fingers, await Kim's ministrations.
When and from where did each arrive?
Did they dock by night, huddled
in a boat's hull? Or breeze through
Kennedy Airport into the arms of relatives?

A young woman at the back sips noodle soup,
its steam mixed with lacquer fumes.

From a white-and-gold plastic frame,
twelve apostles gather for their last meal.
Jesus holds out his calloused hands.

Tableau

You,   me,   a stranger.

Cedar trees sway and touch,
the bay glitters implausibly.

We have traversed a field, swings,
and baseball diamond to reach this grove

    deserted

except   for   us.

The stranger sits atop a picnic table,
phone in hand, protesting,

You don't understand what I mean.

You walk away from me,
reach inside your pocket: Flash of silver.

  Your moving lips.   I move

    away from you,

speed-dial, face the blue beyond,
    wait
for a connection.

    The stranger buries
his face in his hands.

Travels Inside a Cloister Off Ninth Avenue

Wrens flit through the elms. They appear,
disappear, undwarfed by the immense
rooms, announcing themselves, at home
in their journeys.

Rood screen at the altar:
I can name every apostle but one.
Who is this who holds a horse's reins,
just arrived or just about to go? And how far
did the light travel to pour itself through
red-orange glass, little fire of hope landed
at my feet? Backwards the light moves
to its source, a sequence of beginnings,
endings, beginnings: Eve tempted by the serpent,
banishment, the Last Supper.

Propped behind the last pew, a massive book lies
open to "Petitions for the Sick." I scrawl my name
on a blank page and leave myself there,
crawling across the desert.

Missing the Names

Not to know the names of birds
who call to one another
guttural or tuneful through trees,

or the name of the tree
from which this leaf drifted down,
that I pick up to inspect—
ashy underside exposed, spiraling
to a tight brown corkscrew at its tip,

reminding me of native hats I've seen
in photos of a distant people,
who live, I think, somewhere
in the mountains of Asia, maybe Bhutan,
maybe I can find them,

not to know the name of every nation
in Asia, Africa, South America, the world
in flux, the names of nations changing
as people revolt and take aim,
while impossibly brilliant birds squawk above
plazas and plains, the bloodied nameless.

The Office

Fractured words
in Books of many Faces.
Fractiousness
beyond the cubicle
a constant buzz.

I data-mine for meaning,
believing
it's there to be found.
I'm a prospector shaking his pan,
ever hopeful.

I impersonate Dickinson
in my email to a stranger,
stepping aside to let Death
pass by on my way back

to my Home Sweet,
my cyber cabinette,
to My Space
and no one else's.

Across the Gulf

Raised eyebrows make him roar
with laughter, so I greet him
in his wheelchair, do my best
Groucho Marx routine, minus

the cigar. May I please have more
than my father's toothless laughter?
May I have his jokes back, stories, puns,
scrabble games, him? But he's gone blank

again—a book closed on a muddled tale.
Why? I ask myself, brows lifting.
Watching me, he throws his head back,
a boy convulsed with a boy's joy,

and I seize his cold hand,
point outside the picture windows
in the lounge to the clouds that blush,
then rush off into the dark,

blur of yellow cabs, three kids tossing a ball.
Look, Dad, see this and this and this.
Sometimes he nods off. Sometimes he nods
assent and can stutter the words

across the gulf of 35th Avenue:
*Mex-i-can Cof-fee Shop, Hap-py
Pe-king Kit-chen*, and when he does,
my eyebrows shoot up again, pleading

for more, may I please have more father,
oh please, and the overturned bowls
of my cheeks nearly crack
in the laughter and the asking.

Introducing the Forest to Vivaldi

Ignore the crows, their rude calls from the balcony
of trees. This concert piped through speakers
isn't meant for them but you: dulcet chorus of vireos,
cardinals, wrens, doves, whose daily rhapsody
goes unapplauded. Allow yourselves a brief
intermission and settle into plush evergreen.
Listen to the strings and flutes, how they seem
to imitate you in their fluttering grief
and patient beseeching. But how can
we match a music of constant hunger and quick
relief, your allegro heartbeat, life a short, lit wick?
If this serenade can offer any lesson,
it will be after the last note, when silence swells
your throats with its hum and seeps
into folded wings like the moment before sleep.

Frigid the Room of Blue Light

and its assembly, genderless and mouthless
in blue gowns and masks, actors
in the theater of medicine. Prompted,
I recite my lines, state and sign
my name to the ice-white paper thrust
before my face, state my DOB,
first appearance in a room
not unlike this one.
How many times in 13 months
did I enter the blue light
that knocked me out and into
the world of not knowing?
Eight times. Eight times wheeled
through a door that sealed shut
that cold flesh-locker
of blue light, zone of sharp
tools, blood, and banter
that I'd hear as if from a distance,
just before the knowing returned.

Lace

In small Mediterranean towns
women, stooped, and girls
with rag-soft bodies
are making lace intricate as brain circuitry.

See how the light spins through,
imprinting the wall—
not with a maze, but a map
to trace your way home

to women yet unborn who'll find
the lace at the bottom of a cedar chest,
and marvel.

When the world is like a skein
unraveling, look again to the lace: see
how absence forms its pattern,
and purpose fills even the smallest space.

Similes in Late August, 2011

Red fans out from darkening clouds
like spikes on the Statue of Liberty's crown,
my husband says, gazing from our window.
I'm surprised, but touched, by the path
his mind still takes. He conjures nobility,
I conjure apocalypse—warriors who take aim
and thrust their bloody weapons until clouds
shroud them from view.

This is what it feels like to stand at the end
of summer in a new century already careening
toward the edge, searching for signs
while the latest device vibrates messages
against my skin—fearing the seers' predictions,
that it's just a matter of time
before the sky topples into this kitchen,
piercing the heart of us.

Giraffes, Once Dismissed As Mute,

speak in a frequency

too low for us to hear,

conversing in their own

music of the spheres—

just as the stripped trees,

comatose we think,

might be humming

sprightly tunes to one another

on a cracked-ice night

such as this as we lie trussed

in blankets, awake

to the huffing of snow,

syncopation

of winter-weary hearts.

A Facebook Page in Iran

It's raining Farsi here, so hard
I can't see my way

through a fog of curlicues.
I bump into Mohsen, trapped

there and he knows it. He knows
the official no-no's, too many to list,

but his page is Fort Defiance,
I'm guessing, each post a tinderbox

of revolution and rock 'n roll, mixed in
with pix of friends looking weird but smart,

rueful smiles from cafes. I'm no code-breaker,
but I'm working on it. When Whitney died,

the message was clear: he mourned
in heartbroken English,

a rant that out-roared oceans,
and I wanted to say: oh yahoo dot com friend,

oh Rumi-quoting poet, oh beardless infidel,
post and post again to burn the tyrant's Rulebook.

The Tatted Handkerchief

From Elena, Bill's mother,
this linen square edged with tatting—
a wedding present I'd forsaken
for decades in a cardboard box.

I hold it to my face now, trying
to inhale the history of women's lives,
to understand at last this gift
she'd sewn as a girl under the gaze
of her immigrant mother—"Dead
from a hemorrhage at forty-five,"
she whispered, light draining from the room.

Elena's mother looked out from her frame
in gentle reproach, a thin-lipped Cassandra
resigned to her own fate. We were alone
and I was just 20, perplexed
by this gift weighted with grief.
Exchanging vows with her son
soon after, I remember how white fluttered
before Elena's face like a small bird awakening.

I examine the handkerchief,
unfrayed and unfaded, admire
its intricate loops of lilac and lemon yellow.
Were they colors the mother chose for the girl,
recalling San Mauro Forte's hills in spring?
The tatted circles climb three tiers high,
each knot intact, thread joined to thread

like the fingers of a family of acrobats
stretched to hold one another,
defy expectation, achieve a tenuous balance.

Pastorale

In the war game of chess,
kings and pawns know their place
on the board and space
themselves neatly apart. Mess

is not the military way
of course, which is why the field
around my brother's house, filled
with vintage army trucks, stayed

regimentally calm. Still,
there was something disquieting
to see all that armor fight
for attention, vying with frilly

ferns among the lilies, the kind
that bloom and die in a single
day. Visiting, I'd raise two fingers
in salute—half in jest to rile

Bob, but half in deference
to war's mysterious, lifelong grip
on him, a child conscript.
Our worried parents held conferences

on what might be the cause,
then gave up, bought him *Jane's
Fighting Ships* as a birthday gift. Insane—
a boy of eight who knew the force

of every Gatling gun and quoted
General Patton by heart. The radio van,
Vietnam jeep and cargo truck, crammed
once with men, have long been sold.

Only armored beetles live there
now. I imagine them in a march
to his shed where even parched,
dusty air can't dull the glare

of cherished brass: mortar shells
from our father's war lined
up by size in gleaming rows. Find
out the reason he clings to this. *Tell*

me why! Our voices rise, echo
present and past in this valley—
like ricochets that sully
the air, or words ending in blows.

On New Year's Eve

Snow arrives unannounced,
ragged beggar at my window.
      Go away.
I'm reading a letter just arrived
from my lost childhood friend;
white tatters fly at me sideways
like shredded mail escaped
from a slit trash bag.

I'm thinking of words missing
and found (those scattered
love letters we recovered
from the sidewalk and pored over,
two girls peeking
through a stranger's window).

I'm remembering the joy that June day
of our shouted countdown to zero,
ripping stacks of freshman exams,
tearing all those questions
into words, letters, fractured type-strokes,
our ecstatic new language
of confetti, soon wind-scattered
into gutters and pavement cracks.

I'm pondering the decades of our hesitations
and silences, what the world will cast off
and count down tonight,
the rags-to-riches eloquence
of snow heaps.

Two Doors

Manuscripts at the Pierpont Morgan Library

A trellis of golden vines
entwined around the letter A—
in the Middle Ages, stories began
at the beginning, a life painted
and compressed inside a few small squares
that followed, one after the next,
like doors opening to a citadel

of light. Responding to George Plimpton's invitation
to be interviewed by *The Paris Review*
on the art of fiction, Ernest Hemingway
writes from the Ritz in Le Ville Lumière, "Fuck
the art of fiction," but thinks better
of slamming the door shut, and, in four pages,
charms his way back into his future.

A Hologram State of Mind

That glass of wine suspended in air
decades ago—3-D projection still a tactile
memory, the ruby liquid shimmering
as if just poured into its goblet,
the hands reaching out,
all of us incredulous then believing
before this chalice raised to science and art.

And now in Japan, rising pop diva
cat-girl Hatsune Miku—a high-def,
green-haired avatar—"sings"
synthesized pop in huge stadiums,
bloodless and breathless
for thousands of fans.

Today as the self-described
"philosopher of blogging" lectured,
the word *virtual*
crawled off the Power Point screen
over his skin, and I wondered
if he knew what we saw
and what we believed was true.

Now a Chill Replaces the Light

Snow slips off its lustrous sheath,
   shimmies into black, merges
      with air—you know, that slick
         magic act. I turn on every lamp,

grateful for hundred-watt fires.
   There are no stars tonight
      to demand homage
         before their cold and distant

silence: tonight, only
   the immeasurable spaces
      between them and a need
         expressed with a negative:

not to be invisible. So I'm making
   what I can against the hours:
      this bed strewn with poems
         ripped from magazines,

these blue tracks across white tundra
   that my pen may follow,
      this smoky wisp
         rising from somewhere.

ABOUT THE AUTHOR

MARIA TERRONE is the author of *A Secret Room in Fall* (McGovern Award, Ashland Poetry Press), *The Bodies We Were Loaned* (The Word Works), the chapbook *American Gothic, Take 2* (Finishing Line Press), and now, *Eye to Eye* (Bordighera Press). Her poetry, which has been published in French and Farsi and nominated four times for a Pushcart Prize, has appeared in magazines such as *Poetry, Ploughshares, Hudson Review, Poetry International,* and *Crab Orchard Review.* She is the recipient of the Mathiasen Award; Elinor Benedict Prize in Poetry; Allen Tate Memorial Award; and Willow Review Award in Poetry.

Her poems appear in more than 20 anthologies from publishers including the Alfred A. Knopf Everyman's Library, CavanKerry Press, The Feminist Press and Beacon Press. In 2012, Maria Terrone was one of 10 Queens-based writers commissioned by the Guggenheim Museum for its project, "stillspotting nyc."

A native New Yorker, she works as a communications consultant for higher education and lives in Queens with her husband, Bill. Visit her at www.mariaterrone.com, a site made possible by an Individual Artist Initiative Award from the Queens Council on the Arts.

VIA FOLIOS
A refereed book series dedicated to the culture of Italians and Italian Americans.

CONSTANCE SANCETTA. *Here in Cerchio* Vol 93 Local History. $15
MARIA MAZZIOTTI GILLAN. *Ancestors' Song* Vol 92 Poetry. $14
DARRELL FUSARO. *What if Godzilla Just Wanted a Hug?* Vol ? Essays. $TBA
MICHAEL PARENTI. *Waiting for Yesterday: Pages from a Street Kid's Life.* Vol 90 Memoir. $15
ANNIE LANZILOTTO, *Schistsong*, Vol. 89. Poetry, $15
EMANUEL DI PASQUALE, *Love Lines*, Vol. 88. Poetry, $10
CAROSONE & LOGIUDICE. *Our Naked Lives.* Vol 87 Essays. $15
JAMES PERICONI. *Strangers in a Strange Land: A Survey of Italian-Language American Books.* Vol. 86. Book History. $24
DANIELA GIOSEFFI, *Escaping La Vita Della Cucina*, Vol. 85. Essays & Creative Writing. $22
MARIA FAMÀ, *Mystics in the Family*, Vol. 84. Poetry, $10
ROSSANA DEL ZIO, *From Bread and Tomatoes to Zuppa di Pesce "Ciambotto"*, Vol. 83. $15
LORENZO DELBOCA, *Polentoni*, Vol. 82. Italian Studies, $15
SAMUEL GHELLI, *A Reference Grammar*, Vol. 81. Italian Language. $36
ROSS TALARICO, *Sled Run*, Vol. 80. Fiction. $15
FRED MISURELLA, *Only Sons*, Vol. 79. Fiction. $14
FRANK LENTRICCHIA, *The Portable Lentricchia*, Vol. 78. Fiction. $16
RICHARD VETERE, *The Other Colors in a Snow Storm*, Vol. 77. Poetry. $10
GARIBALDI LAPOLLA, *Fire in the Flesh*, Vol. 76 Fiction & Criticism. $25
GEORGE GUIDA, *The Pope Stories*, Vol. 75 Prose. $15
ROBERT VISCUSI, *Ellis Island*, Vol. 74. Poetry. $28
ELENA GIANINI BELOTTI, *The Bitter Taste of Strangers Bread*, Vol. 73, Fiction, $24
PINO APRILE, *Terroni*, Vol. 72, Italian Studies, $20
EMANUEL DI PASQUALE, *Harvest*, Vol. 71, Poetry, $10
ROBERT ZWEIG, *Return to Naples*, Vol. 70, Memoir, $16
AIROS & CAPPELLI, *Guido*, Vol. 69, Italian/American Studies, $12
FRED GARDAPHÉ, *Moustache Pete is Dead! Long Live Moustache Pete!*, Vol. 67, Literature/Oral History, $12
PAOLO RUFFILLI, *Dark Room/Camera oscura*, Vol. 66, Poetry, $11
HELEN BAROLINI, *Crossing the Alps*, Vol. 65, Fiction, $14
COSMO FERRARA, *Profiles of Italian Americans*, Vol. 64, Italian Americana, $16
GIL FAGIANI, *Chianti in Connecticut*, Vol. 63, Poetry, $10
BASSETTI & D'ACQUINO, *Italic Lessons*, Vol. 62, Italian/American Studies, $10
CAVALIERI & PASCARELLI, Eds., *The Poet's Cookbook*, Vol. 61, Poetry/Recipes, $12
EMANUEL DI PASQUALE, *Siciliana*, Vol. 60, Poetry, $8
NATALIA COSTA, Ed., *Bufalini*, Vol. 59, Poetry. $18.
RICHARD VETERE, *Baroque*, Vol. 58, Fiction. $18.
LEWIS TURCO, *La Famiglia/The Family*, Vol. 57, Memoir, $15
NICK JAMES MILETI, *The Unscrupulous*, Vol. 56, Humanities, $20
BASSETTI, ACCOLLA, D'AQUINO, *Italici: An Encounter with Piero Bassetti*, Vol. 55, Italian Studies, $8
GIOSE RIMANELLI, *The Three-legged One*, Vol. 54, Fiction, $15
CHARLES KLOPP, *Bele Antiche Stòrie*, Vol. 53, Criticism, $25
JOSEPH RICAPITO, *Second Wave*, Vol. 52, Poetry, $12

Bordighera Press is an imprint of Bordighera, Incorporated, an independently owned not-for-profit scholarly organization that has no legal affiliation with the University of Central Florida or with The John D. Calandra Italian American Institute, Queens College/CUNY.

GARY MORMINO, *Italians in Florida*, Vol. 51, History, $15
GIANFRANCO ANGELUCCI, *Federico F.*, Vol. 50, Fiction, $15
ANTHONY VALERIO, *The Little Sailor*, Vol. 49, Memoir, $9
ROSS TALARICO, *The Reptilian Interludes*, Vol. 48, Poetry, $15
RACHEL GUIDO DE VRIES, *Teeny Tiny Tino's Fishing Story*, Vol. 47, Children's Literature, $6
EMANUEL DI PASQUALE, *Writing Anew*, Vol. 46, Poetry, $15
MARIA FAMÀ, *Looking For Cover*, Vol. 45, Poetry, $12
ANTHONY VALERIO, *Toni Cade Bambara's One Sicilian Night*, Vol. 44, Poetry, $10
EMANUEL CARNEVALI, Dennis Barone, Ed., *Furnished Rooms*, Vol. 43, Poetry, $14
BRENT ADKINS, et al., Ed., *Shifting Borders, Negotiating Places*, Vol. 42, Proceedings, $18
GEORGE GUIDA, *Low Italian*, Vol. 41, Poetry, $11
GARDAPHÈ, GIORDANO, TAMBURRI, *Introducing Italian Americana*, Vol. 40, Italian/American Studies, $10
DANIELA GIOSEFFI, *Blood Autumn/Autunno di sangue*, Vol. 39, Poetry, $15/$25
FRED MISURELLA, *Lies to Live by*, Vol. 38, Stories, $15
STEVEN BELLUSCIO, *Constructing a Bibliography*, Vol. 37, Italian Americana, $15
ANTHONY JULIAN TAMBURRI, Ed., *Italian Cultural Studies 2002*, Vol. 36, Essays, $18
BEA TUSIANI, *con amore*, Vol. 35, Memoir, $19
FLAVIA BRIZIO-SKOV, Ed., *Reconstructing Societies in the Aftermath of War*, Vol. 34, History, $30
TAMBURRI, et al., Eds., *Italian Cultural Studies 2001*, Vol. 33, Essays, $18
ELIZABETH G. MESSINA, Ed., *In Our Own Voices*, Vol. 32, Italian/American Studies, $25
STANISLAO G. PUGLIESE, *Desperate Inscriptions*, Vol. 31, History, $12
HOSTERT & TAMBURRI, Eds., *Screening Ethnicity*, Vol. 30, Italian/American Culture, $25
G. PARATI & B. LAWTON, Eds., *Italian Cultural Studies*, Vol. 29, Essays, $18
HELEN BAROLINI, *More Italian Hours*, Vol. 28, Fiction, $16
FRANCO NASI, Ed., *Intorno alla Via Emilia*, Vol. 27, Culture, $16
ARTHUR L. CLEMENTS, *The Book of Madness & Love*, Vol. 26, Poetry, $10
JOHN CASEY, et al., *Imagining Humanity*, Vol. 25, Interdisciplinary Studies, $18
ROBERT LIMA, *Sardinia/Sardegna*, Vol. 24, Poetry, $10
DANIELA GIOSEFFI, *Going On*, Vol. 23, Poetry, $10
ROSS TALARICO, *The Journey Home*, Vol. 22, Poetry, $12
EMANUEL DI PASQUALE, *The Silver Lake Love Poems*, Vol. 21, Poetry, $7
JOSEPH TUSIANI, *Ethnicity*, Vol. 20, Poetry, $12
JENNIFER LAGIER, *Second Class Citizen*, Vol. 19, Poetry, $8
FELIX STEFANILE, *The Country of Absence*, Vol. 18, Poetry, $9
PHILIP CANNISTRARO, *Blackshirts*, Vol. 17, History, $12
LUIGI RUSTICHELLI, Ed., *Seminario sul racconto*, Vol. 16, Narrative, $10
LEWIS TURCO, *Shaking the Family Tree*, Vol. 15, Memoirs, $9
LUIGI RUSTICHELLI, Ed., *Seminario sulla drammaturgia*, Vol. 14, Theater/Essays, $10
FRED GARDAPHÈ, *Moustache Pete is Dead! Long Live Moustache Pete!*, Vol. 13, Oral Literature, $10
JONE GAILLARD CORSI, *Il libretto d'autore*, 1860–1930, Vol. 12, Criticism, $17
HELEN BAROLINI, *Chiaroscuro: Essays of Identity*, Vol. 11, Essays, $15
PICARAZZI & FEINSTEIN, Eds., *An African Harlequin in Milan*, Vol. 10, Theater/Essays, $15
JOSEPH RICAPITO, *Florentine Streets & Other Poems*, Vol. 9, Poetry, $9
FRED MISURELLA, *Short Time*, Vol. 8, Novella, $7
NED CONDINI, *Quartettsatz*, Vol. 7, Poetry, $7
ANTHONY JULIAN TAMBURRI, Ed., *Fuori: Essays by Italian/American Lesbians and Gays*, Vol. 6, Essays, $10
ANTONIO GRAMSCI, P. Verdicchio, Trans. & Intro., *The Southern Question*, Vol. 5, Social Criticism, $5

DANIELA GIOSEFFI, *Word Wounds & Water Flowers*, Vol. 4, Poetry, $8
WILEY FEINSTEIN, *Humility's Deceit: Calvino Reading Ariosto Reading Calvino*, Vol. 3, Criticism, $10
PAOLO A. GIORDANO, Ed., *Joseph Tusiani: Poet, Translator, Humanist*, Vol. 2, Criticism, $25
ROBERT VISCUSI, *Oration Upon the Most Recent Death of Christopher Columbus*, Vol. 1, Poetry, $3

www.ingramcontent.com/pod-product-compliance
Lightning Source LLC
Chambersburg PA
CBHW020942090426
42736CB00010B/1235